INTRODUCTI

The idea of a list in praise of the world's wonders dates back at least 2,400 years to the writings of the ancient Greek historian, Herodotus. *A Collection of Wonders Around the World* was written by Callimachus, the chief librarian at the Library of Alexandria in Egypt, sometime in the third century B.C.E. but was lost when the library was burned down. The next known mention appears in a poem by Antipater of Sidon written in the second century B.C.E. Antipater mentions six of the wonders found on the list finally compiled in the Middle Ages and still recognized today as the Seven Wonders of the Ancient World:

1. Great Pyramid of Giza
2. Hanging Gardens of Babylon
3. Statue of Zeus at Olympia
4. Temple of Artemis at Ephesus
5. Mausoleum at Halicarnassus
6. Colossus of Rhodes
7. Lighthouse of Alexandria

The only one of the ancient wonders still standing is the Great Pyramid of Giza, completed around 2560 B.C.E. as a tomb for the Pharaoh Khufu. When Herodotus visited the pyramid, it was encased in 22 acres of polished white Tura limestone, which would have been dazzling in the desert sun. Legend has it that the limestone was later removed by an Arab sultan who had it transported to a construction site in Cairo.

The Great Pyramid of Giza can be seen at the far right. Perspective and a steeper slope make the central pyramid appear larger, but it is not.

Herodotus also described the city of Babylon (in today's Iraq) and its massive walls, which he said were more than 300 feet high and 75 feet thick. "In addition to its size," he wrote, "Babylon surpasses in splendor any city in the known world." He did not, however, mention the Hanging Gardens, which were supposed to have been built in the sixth century B.C.E. by King Nebuchadnezzar II for his wife, who missed her lush and mountainous homeland.

A sculpture of the Greek historian Herodotus (ca. 485–425 B.C.E.).

According to the many descriptions that have been written since Herodotus, the gardens were built in large, stepped terraces that rose 450 feet above the banks of the Euphrates River. Each level was connected by marble stairways and planted with overhanging trees and bushes. Despite all the descriptions, no mention of the gardens has been found in contemporary Babylonian records. Whether or not the gardens really existed is still an open question.

The first recorded Olympic Games took place in 776 B.C.E. in Olympia, about 90 miles west of Athens, Greece. As the Games gained in popularity and importance, a splendid temple was built for Zeus, the most important Greek god in whose honor, legend has it, the Games were first staged by his son Herakles. The sculptor Pheidias was commissioned to create a statue of Zeus for the inside of the temple.

On site, Pheidias erected a wood frame that he would cover with sheets of ivory and gold that he carved in his workshop. When completed, the 40-foot-tall statue of Zeus sat on a throne of cedar inlaid with ivory, ebony, and gold. A Greek historian named Strabo wrote that Zeus was so large, it seemed like he would break through the ceiling of the temple should he stand up.

There were eight gates in the walls surrounding the city of Babylon. Shown here is a reconstruction of the Ishtar Gate.

For more than 800 years, the statue was seen by thousands of people who traveled to Olympia for the Games. Then in C.E. 391, the Games were banned and the temple closed by the Christian emperor Theodosius I. Eventually, the statue was moved to a palace in today's Istanbul, where it stood until destroyed by fire in the fifth century C.E.

In Greece, Artemis was the goddess of the hunt and the moon, but in Ephesus (in modern-day Turkey), she was a goddess of fertility. Several temples were built in her honor at Ephesus, one of which was burned down in 356 B.C.E. by a man named Herostratus, who set the temple on fire so that he would be remembered throughout history. Afterward, the temple was rebuilt and eventually became one of the Seven Wonders of the Ancient World.

A woodcut picturing Strabo, a Greek historian.

Constructed entirely of marble, the structure was supported by 127 sixty-foot-tall columns. Scenes were sculpted around the bases of at least 36 of them. Within the temple, some of the columns were covered with gold or silver. Other decorations included paintings and bronze statues of Amazon warriors.

This temple was destroyed in C.E. 262 when Ephesus was raided by the Goths. It was rebuilt once more but is said to have been torn down at the behest of St. John Chrysostom in C.E. 401. Afterward, the city of Ephesus declined and was eventually deserted.

King Maussollos ruled Caria, a part of the Persian Empire, from 377 to 353 B.C.E. His capital was Halicarnassus (today's Bodrum in southeast Turkey). Work was probably begun

The Artemis of Ephesus was depicted with multiple breasts, symbols of fertility, from shoulders to waist.

on his tomb before his death and continued by his queen (and sister), Artemisia, until her death in 351.

The tomb was built atop a hill and, according to the Roman author Pliny the Elder, stood 140 feet high. The base was topped by 36 columns, which supported a roof in the shape of a stepped pyramid. At the very top was a marble chariot pulled by four horses. Other decorations included sculptural portraits of the court, life-size statues depicting hunting and ceremonial scenes, and three friezes, one of them showing a fierce battle between Herakles and the Amazons.

In C.E. 1494, the tomb, which had been damaged by earthquakes, was torn down by crusaders who used the blocks to fortify the huge castle they'd built earlier in the century. Today, visitors to London's British Museum can see remnants of the tomb, among them fragments of statues, some of which have been reconstructed, and several sections of the Amazon frieze. As for Maussollos, his name lives on in the word *mausoleum*, which is still used to describe monumental tombs.

Much as America's Statue of Liberty, dubbed the "modern colossus," greets visitors to New York Harbor, a huge statue once towered over Mandraki Harbor, the entrance to the city of Rhodes on the Greek island of the same name. In fact, Liberty's sculptor, Frédéric Auguste Bartholdi, spoke of finding part of his inspiration in that ancient Colossus.

In 305 B.C.E., Demetrius of Macedonia besieged Rhodes with an army of 40,000, but was unable to capture it. After a year-long struggle, Demetrius gave up and abandoned the island, leaving his siege engines behind. To commemorate their victory, the Rhodians sold the equipment and used the money to build a statue of Helios, god of the sun, who was said to have pulled the island of Rhodes from the sea.

Though often pictured straddling the harbor entrance, as here, the Colossus of Rhodes probably stood on only one side of the harbor.

It took 12 years to build the 110-foot-tall statue, which was made out of bronze supported by a stone and iron framework, and stood on a 50-foot-tall marble base. The Colossus presided over the harbor for just 56 years before it was toppled in an earthquake. The ruins continued to attract visitors until C.E. 654, when Rhodes was conquered by the Arabs. It's said that the ruins were then sold and transported to Syria on the backs of 900 camels.

The world's first lighthouse was built on the island of Pharos in Alexandria, Egypt. It was commissioned by the ruler Ptolemy I in the late third century B.C.E. and completed during the reign of his son, Ptolemy II. It was constructed in three sections: The base was in the shape of a square, the center was octagonal, and the top was circular and crowned by a statue of Poseidon, god of the sea. Altogether, the structure stood almost 400 feet high. During the day, a polished metal mirror reflected the sun's rays and

An 18th-century engraving of the Lighthouse of Alexandria.

at night, the light of fires burning inside the shaft of the top section. The beacon was said to reach 35 miles out to sea.

Legend has it that the lighthouse's designer, Sostrates, wanted his name inscribed at the base of the building. Ptolemy II refused the request, however, wanting only his own name to appear. The clever Sostrates solved his dilemma by engraving his name then covering it with plaster on which he carved Ptolemy's name. Sostrates knew that in time, the plaster would weather away to reveal his own name.

The Lighthouse at Alexandria stood for centuries, but was badly damaged by earthquakes in C.E. 1303 and 1323. Ibn Battuta, the famous Moroccan traveler, visited the lighthouse in 1326 and could still reach the door on the first floor, but by the time he returned in 1349, the lighthouse had collapsed. By 1480, the ruins of the lighthouse had been used to build a fort in its place.

The Grand Canyon

Since the Middle Ages, many other lists have been written, of seven natural wonders, seven modern wonders, seven technological wonders, and more. Why seven? In the beginning, it was probably because the number seven held religious significance. Today, naming seven wonders has become tradition. As this book goes to press, voters will be choosing the New 7 Wonders of the World from a list of 21 finalists culled from 77 nominees. The finalists are all manmade but not necessarily new, and 11 of them are included in this book, which contains 40 wonders, both manmade and natural, from every corner of the Earth.

Usually the type of 3-D effect used in *Wonders of the World* is created with a stereo camera, which has two lenses set no more than 2.5 inches apart. This allows the photographer to take two photos at a time, each from a slightly different perspective. When the photographs are viewed through special lenses, the brain combines the two images into one 3-D image.

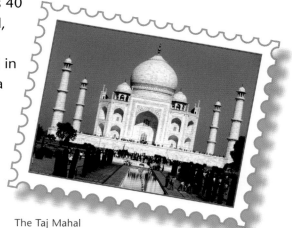

The Taj Mahal

Wonders of the World in 3-D, however, was made with photographs that already existed. To turn the images into stereo pairs, computer programs were used to separate each image into as many as 12 layers. Then each layer was examined to see which ones would work together to make the best 3-D image.

THE IMAGES

LIBERTY ISLAND, NYC

In 1865, sculptor Frédéric Auguste Bartholdi attended a dinner party where the host suggested that France present the United States with a monument to mark the centennial of its founding and celebrate the friendship between the two nations. When the idea became reality, Bartholdi designed a huge statue, which he envisioned standing on an island in New York Harbor. Work began in 1875, with Gustave Eiffel, who would later build the eponymous tower, designing the iron framework that would support the copper statue. Ten years later, the completed statue was dismantled and shipped to New York in 350 sections. After being reassembled on a granite-sheathed concrete pedestal, *Liberty Enlightening the World* was dedicated in October 1886. Lady Liberty carries a torch and wears a crown with one point for each of the seven seas and continents. At her feet are broken shackles, symbolizing freedom from oppression.

Luray Caverns

VIRGINIA

A stunning assortment of shapes and colors decorate the interior of Virginia's Luray Caverns, constituting some of nature's most fanciful work. Discovered in 1878, the caverns were formed millions of years ago. As water seeped though porous rock, it deposited minerals in creative ways, building up a variety of forms. Stalactites hang from ceilings like icicles, while stalagmites form colorful gardens on the cavern floors. Meandering rivers dropped minerals as they evaporated, leaving behind stone formations that look like waterfalls, veils, flowing robes, and even a few animal shapes. In the 1950s, a mathematician named Leland Sprinkle selected stalactites throughout the 3.5-acre site to match the musical scale, creating the world's largest musical instrument, an organ whose stalactite pipes fill the caverns with song.

Mount Rushmore

BLACK HILLS, SOUTH DAKOTA

Gutzon Borglum was already an established artist when South Dakota officials invited him to create a colossal sculpture that would become "a gateway to the west." For his site, Borglum selected Mount Rushmore, a granite peak with an exposure that ensured his creation would be sunlit for most of the day. Four presidents were chosen: founding father George Washington; Thomas Jefferson, architect of the Louisiana Purchase; Abraham Lincoln, emancipator and preserver of the union; and Theodore Roosevelt, whose bold, adventurous nature epitomized the spirit of America.

Carving on the 60-foot-high heads of the world's largest sculpture began in 1927 and continued for 14 years. Workers used dynamite to remove the granite to within inches of the finished surface. Then, in a process called honeycombing, they closely drilled holes to weaken the remaining rock so it could be easily removed. Finally, they smoothed the surface using drills with a special bit.

MANITOBA, CANADA

Most often visible from September to October and from March to April, the northern lights are also known as the aurora borealis (Latin for "northern dawn"). This spellbinding show appears in the sky as a multihued curtain of glowing light.

The aurora is caused by disruptions in the solar wind, charged particles emitted by the sun. Normally, Earth's magnetic field deflects the solar wind. When distubances such as solar flares occur on the sun, however, the charged particles follow lines of magnetic force into the upper atmosphere near the north and south poles. The energy produced by the collision of the charged particles with the atoms and molecules of the atmosphere results in the aurora. In the southern hemisphere, the phenomenon is called the southern lights or aurora australis ("southern dawn").

UTAH

Spanning 275 feet and reaching a height of 290 feet, Rainbow Bridge is the world's largest known natural bridge. Long a sacred place to Native Americans, particularly the Navajo, its existence was not known to the world at large until 1909, when a government expedition came across the spectacular rock formation on horseback. A year later, President William Howard Taft declared Rainbow Bridge a national monument.

A testament to the powerful force of water, the bridge was sculpted by a stream that cut a hole through the rock about five million years ago. Rainbow Bridge is composed of various layers and shades of sandstone, whose colors are made even more brilliant at sunset.

ARIZONA

Water and ice played the biggest roles in the formation of the Grand Canyon. In winter, ice widens cracks in the rock, eventually breaking it apart. Heavy rains and snowmelt from the Rocky Mountains flood down side canyons, picking up dirt, loose rock, and even huge boulders, and dumping them into the Colorado River. During spring floods, the Colorado once flowed more than 100,000 cubic feet per second, its debris scouring both riverbanks and riverbed as it cut down through the Colorado Plateau. Today, the Grand Canyon is 277 miles long and averages 4,000 feet deep along its entire length, reaching 6,000 feet at its deepest point. Its walls are composed of almost 40 different layers of rock, many of which were formed by the advance and retreat of ancient seas long before the canyon came into being about five or six million years ago.

CALIFORNIA

To protect the area from developers, President Abraham Lincoln signed a bill on June 30, 1864, designating land in and around the Yosemite Valley to be held in an inalienable public trust. This marked the first time ever that a federal government set aside scenic land for the enjoyment of all of its citizens. In 1872, Yellowstone became America's first official national park.

Encompassing 1,200 square miles of pristine land, the park is known for its spectacular granite cliffs, waterfalls, and streams as well as for its majestic sequoias. Yellowstone contains five vegetation zones, ranging from the foothill woodland zone at about 1,800 feet above sea level to the alpine zone, which begins at around 9,500 feet. Together, they support more than 1,500 species of plants and 250 species of vertebrate animals, including black bears, bobcats, and mountain lions.

SAN FRANCISCO, CALIFORNIA

Until the Golden Gate Bridge was built, no one had ever attempted to sink a tower foundation pier 100 feet beneath the churning waters of an open sea. Yet the challenge was met brilliantly by its engineer, Joseph Strauss. This marvel of engineering, with its 746-foot-tall towers, 3-foot-thick main cables, and massive underwater structure, has withstood earthquakes, high winds, and raging water currents, not to mention heavy traffic: Over 45 million vehicles cross over it annually. At its completion in 1937, the Golden Gate was the longest suspension bridge in the world, a record it held until 1964 when New York's Verrazano-Narrows Bridge was built. Considered one of the world's most beautiful bridges, the Golden Gate spans just over a mile, linking the city of San Francisco with Marin County.

Chichén Itzá

While Europe was immersed in the Dark Ages, another civilization was reaching its zenith. The Maya civilization extended from southern Mexico through Central America and boasted sophisticated accomplishments in mathematics, astronomy, and architecture. Remains of a Maya city can be seen at Chichén Itzá. Built about C.E. 1050, the Temple of Kulkulkan (also known as Quetzalcoatl) is a four-sided stepped pyramid that towers 79 feet above the ruins. The pyramid served as a solar calendar, with 91 steps on each side. An added step at the top brings the total to 365 steps—one for each day of the year. At both the spring and autumn equinoxes, the sun shining on the pyramid's main stairway creates shadows that give the illusion of a snake slithering down the stairs to the carved serpent's head at the bottom. The sculpture in the foreground of the photo is a chacmool, a type of stone altar.

Machu Picchu

High on a ridge above the Urubamba River canyon, the small Incan city of Machu Picchu lies hidden almost 8,000 feet above sea level. Built in the mid-1400s, this extraordinary archaeological complex was never found by the Spanish conquistadors who arrived in 1532. Machu Picchu's 200-odd buildings were mostly homes, but there were also temples and other public buildings, often built with blocks of stone fitted tightly together without mortar. Alleyways, side streets, and more than 100 stairways connected all sections of the city. On the outskirts were irrigated terraces where crops were grown and stables where livestock were kept. Still standing is the city's *intihuatana* stone, a column used during the spring and fall equinoxes to "tie" the sun to the Earth and prevent it from moving further in the sky. Because the Incas left no writing, however, much of the inhabitants' lives remain as shrouded in mystery as the thick mountain mist that often hovers over the city's ruins.

Rio de Janeiro

This stunning city combines elements of the most admired landscapes: rocky cliffs, lush green mountains, stunning architecture, and a magnificent harbor. Legend has it that when the Portuguese explorer Gaspar de Lemos first arrived in the area on January 20, 1502, he thought he had sailed into the mouth of a huge river, so he named the region *Rio de Janeiro*, or "River of January." In fact, the harbor is on the southwestern shore of Guanabara Bay. From the summit of Corcovado mountain, topped by the giant statue called *Christ the Redeemer*, the view of the harbor is unparalleled. Out of the dark blue waters jut rocky outcrops, the best known of which is Sugar Loaf Mountain. The harbor is studded with sailing ships and flanked by idyllic beaches including Ipanema and Copacabana. It's no wonder that the locals are fond of saying, "God made the world in six days, and devoted the seventh to creating Rio."

PATAGONIA, CHILE

ocated in the southernmost part of South America, more than 1,500 miles south of Santiago, the capital of Chile, Torres del Paine is widely regarded as one of the most visually stunning, unspoiled places on the planet. Officially declared a Biosphere Reserve in 1978, the park encompasses a wide variety of ecosystems, including a mountain range, pristine lakes, and lush coastal wetlands that support a huge variety of animal and plant life. Torres del Paine takes its name from three sheer granite towers and, at 10,006 feet above sea level, its highest peak is the Paine Grande, but the picturesque Cuernos del Paine, shown rising beyond one of the park's lakes, are the peaks most often photographed as representative of this spectacularly wild and beautiful landscape.

PAGE
32

SCOTIA SEA, ANTARCTICA

C onsisting of a half million years of snow, Antarctica's continental glacier covers more than 5 million square miles of land. Every summer, from December through February, the glacier calves thousands of icebergs, which crash into the sea and drift northward. Some of these icebergs are huge; one observed in 2002 was larger than Maryland. Despite their size, icebergs float because they are less dense than water. The difference is so small, however, that only about 10 percent of an iceberg shows above the waterline.

The iceberg pictured probably came from deep within the glacier, where it was under so much pressure for such a long time that all the air was squeezed out of it. This results in clear ice, which, when struck by light, filters out all the colors in the spectrum except blue. The iceberg's otherworldly shapes were sculpted by wave action, and it's possible that it may have turned over at least once. Hanging out on the iceberg are chinstrap and Adélie penguins.

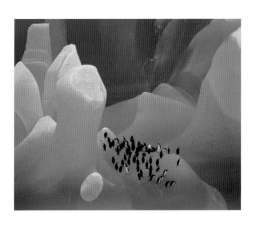

Moai Sculptures

Massive stone sculptures called moai are evidence that a Polynesian culture once flourished on this remote Pacific island, which lies about 2,000 miles west of Chile. Most of the moai were carved from about 1100 to 1650 from the walls of the crater of Rano Raraku, an extinct volcano. They were then moved around the island, possibly by gangs of people pulling them on sledges atop log rollers. The logs and rope came from forests that were eventually decimated by slash-and-burn agriculture. Only about a third of the moai, which represented powerful chiefs and served as conduits to the gods, were erected on shrines called *ahu*, where the statues stood, their backs to the sea. The rest of moai lie in the quarry or along the roads of the island. The average moai weighs about 14 tons and stands over 13 feet tall. However, one statue still attached to the quarry wall is more than 70 feet tall and weighs about 270 tons.

KORO SEA, FIJI

Coral reefs are created by millions of creatures called polyps, which secrete calcium carbonate to form the calyxes, or cups, where the tiny animals take shelter. Attached by means of a self-made connecting tissue, they form ever-growing colonies that come in a variety of shapes. Each polyp has a stomach that is only open at one end—the mouth, which is surrounded by tentacles containing stinging cells used to capture prey. The bright colors of reef-building corals come from a type of algae that lives within the polyps. The algae produce oxygen and help remove wastes in return for protection and nutrients.

The Namena Barrier Reef surrounds Fiji's Namena Island. Covering more than 30 miles, the island, along with its lagoon and reef, were declared a marine reserve in 2003. The reef supports an abundance of fish and invertebrates, while the island provides nesting grounds for sea turtles and red-footed boobies.

Sydney Opera House

AUSTRALIA

Since it opened in 1973, the Sydney Opera House has become one of the most widely recognized buildings in the world as well as the foremost iconic symbol of Australia. Situated on Bennelong Point, a strip of land that reaches out into Sydney Harbor, the building seems poised to take off, like a ship about to set sail. It has been argued that Danish architect Jorn Utzon's design was beyond the technical capabilities of the time. Indeed, it took many attempts through trial and error to achieve the present form of its shells, employing the earliest uses of computer technology. Covering 4.5 acres of land, the opera house is supported by 580 concrete piers. The roof is composed of more than 2,000 pre-cast concrete sections and is covered with over a million self-cleaning Swedish-made tiles.

JAVA, INDONESIA

L ying at the southern end of a long volcanic massif, the erupting Mount Semeru towers over the smaller cones of Bromo (at left) and Batok (foreground). At 12,060 feet above sea level, Semeru is Java's highest volcano as well as its most active. Since 1818, it has erupted 55 times. The most recent eruption began in 1967 and has continued ever since, killing more than 500 people. At times, minor eruptions can occur as often as every 20 to 40 minutes, with the volcano spewing dust and steam high into the air. The display is most spectacular when the steamy cloud is touched by the rays of the sun, creating a kaleidoscope of color above the crater.

JAVA, INDONESIA

onstructed between C.E. 760 and 830, the "mountain of a thousand statues" stands on a plateau in the center of Java. Long abandoned, the temple had become legend by 1814, when an expedition mounted by Sir Thomas Raffles, the British governor of the island, found the site. Almost two million blocks of volcanic stone were used to build the 95-foot-high stepped pyramid, which is the world's largest Buddhist temple. The hidden base and five lower terraces are rectangular and are carved with more than 3,000 bas-relief panels, most depicting the life and teachings of Buddha. The upper three terraces are concentric circles studded with bell-shaped stupas, each of which once contained a statue of a meditating Buddha. Pilgrims climb to the central stupa on the summit in a clockwise direction, making a symbolic journey through the three levels of Buddhist cosmology from worldly desire to the spiritual enlightenment of nirvana.

Banaue Rice Terraces

More than 2,000 years ago, the Ifugao people used their ingenuity and a few basic tools to begin transforming the steep slopes of their mountain homeland into a wonderland of stepped rice terraces. A complicated system of bamboo pipes delivers water to the young rice plants, with runoff from the upper terraces flowing downhill to the terraces below. Today, many of their descendants continue to farm the land organically in precisely the same way, though most cannot make their living solely from the terraces and recently, the younger generation has begun to migrate to the cities.

Mount Fuji

HONSHU ISLAND, JAPAN

World famous for its instantly recognizable conical peak, Mount Fuji is located at the center of Honshu, about 60 miles southwest of Tokyo. A stratovolcano, Fuji is classified as still active, although it has not erupted since 1707. At 12,388 feet above sea level, it is Japan's highest mountain. Fuji is not only regarded as a national symbol but also as a sacred place, inspiring prose, poetry, and countless works of art throughout history. Neither ropes nor crampons are needed to climb Mount Fuji, and its relatively easy ascent makes it a suitable climb for people of all ages. Nevertheless, ceremonies are regularly held in shrines located at its base to pray for the safety of climbers.

Great Wall of China

Around 656 B.C.E., the Chu State built several walls to repel invasions from the north. These walls later became the first part of the Great Wall of China, which would take another 2,000 years to complete. For more than 4,000 miles, the Great Wall wends its way up and down mountains and across grasslands and deserts. Strongholds were built at key locations and beacon towers were erected at various intervals along the wall where soldiers could communicate by smoke signal with their comrades. In places, visitors can still see the holes that were punched in the Wall so soldiers could shoot their arrows through them. The world's largest manmade structure, the Great Wall of China was hand-constructed of brick and stone by hundreds of thousands of workers. Some of those workers lie buried within it.

Shwedagon Pagoda

According to legend, Myanmar's (Burma's) story of the Shwedagon Pagoda began about 2,500 years ago with two brothers, merchants who traveled to India and met the Buddha. The brothers offered cake and honey balls and in return, the Buddha gave them eight strands of his hair. On their return to Yangon (Rangoon), the ruler of the city built Shwedagon Pagoda at the top of Singuttara Hill to enshrine the hairs. Since then, the pagoda has been enlarged several times, reaching its present height of 326 feet in the 15th century. In the beginning, the pagoda was gilded but over time, the upper parts have been clad in solid gold plates, while the very top of the structure is studded with thousands of diamonds, rubies, and other precious stones.

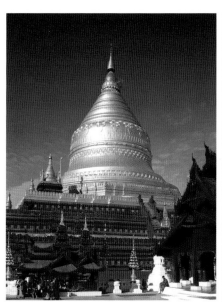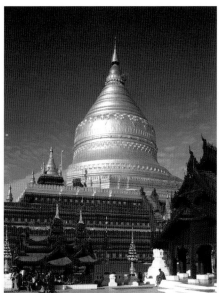

MYANMAR

In Myanmar (Burma), remnants of the ancient kingdom of Bagan rise up on the Eastern bank of the Ayeyarwady (Irrawaddy) River. Like so many sandcastles sparkling in the sun, these elegant shrines to Buddha are a veritable archaeological treasure trove. At one time, Bagan was a thriving city, with 13,000 pagodas and monasteries, most of them built between 1057 and 1287. Today, almost 3,000 of the structures remain. Adorned with intricate carvings, the pagodas are bell-shaped monuments set on square or octagonal bases. The multistoried buildings rise up, tapering to spires often capped by jeweled finials. Inside, corridors covered with beautiful frescoes mingle with sacred shrines and priceless art objects.

AGRA, INDIA

In 1631, Mumtaz Mahal, wife of Indian emperor Shah Jahan, died giving birth to their 14th child. As a tribute to their love, the emperor vowed to build her a tomb of unsurpassable beauty. Few would dispute that he attained his goal. The pure white marble tomb was built on the banks of the Yamuna River. On the opposite side is a classic Islamic-style garden divided by two channels of water that cross in the center. Flanked by four minarets, the tomb sits on a 22-foot-high sandstone platform. Four bisected chambers surround the central dome, giving it an octagonal shape. Almost every surface within and without the Taj Mahal is decorated with delicate carvings, many with inlays of multiple shades of marble and semiprecious stones. Today, the Taj Mahal is widely considered one of the world's most perfect architectural achievements.

GIZA PLATEAU, EGYPT

Three large pyramids stand on the Giza Plateau above Cairo. Still the largest at 449 feet high, the Great Pyramid (far right) once rose to 481 feet. Built for the pharaoh Khufu around the middle of the 26th century B.C.E., it is the only one of the seven wonders of the ancient world still in existence. Recent scholars believe that it took about 30,000 workers 20 years to complete the pyramid, which was created with more than 2.3 million blocks of stone, each weighing about 2.5 tons. Khufu's son Khafra's pyramid (center) was built at a steeper angle than Khufu's, giving the appearance of being larger even though it is not. The smallest of the three pyramids was built by Khafre's son Menkaure, and the even smaller pyramids in the foreground belonged to queens.

ZAMBIA / ZIMBABWE

Sometimes called *Mosi oa Tunya*, which means "the smoke that thunders," Victoria Falls forms a natural barrier between the countries of Zimbabwe and Zambia. At more than a mile wide and up to 350 feet deep in places, Victoria Falls forms the largest curtain of falling water in the world. In fact, the falls are so vast that to grasp their true enormity, the best way to see them is from the air. During the rainy season, more than 17 million cubic feet of water plunge into the narrow chasm, overwhelming the senses with a deafening roar and creating a tower of iridescent mist that can be seen from miles away.

NAMIBIA

Namib means "vast" in the Nama language, and the 55-million-year-old Namib Desert lives up to its name. Running about 300 miles along the Atlantic coast of Namibia, the desert stretches 50 to 125 miles inland. Throughout, rainfall is sparse, averaging under 4 inches per year. Every so often a few of its dry rivers flow, but the waters of only two ever reach the ocean, the others being blocked by sand dunes. The most moisture comes from dense coastal fogs, which occur more than 180 days a year near the ocean.

The Southern Namib is famous for its spectacular sand dunes, which stretch as far as the eye can see and reach elevations of up to 1,000 feet. At sunset, the dunes ignite in shades of blood red, burnt orange, and mauve, creating a fiery landscape of shifting sands that is like no other in the world.

TURKEY

About ten million years ago, the eruptions of three volcanoes in central Turkey covered the area with lava, which formed a thick layer of tufa rock mixed with ash, basalt, and other substances. Over time, wind, rain, and floodwaters carved out a moonscape of soft rock cones and tall mushroom-shaped rock formations often called "fairy chimneys." People began carving dwellings from the rock possibly as long ago as 4000 B.C.E. After the area was Christianized in the first century C.E., underground churches and cities were created to protect communities from invaders and religious persecution. When threatened, whole populations would hide out, sometimes for months, until the danger had passed. Though most of Cappadocia's underground homes have been abandoned, some are still inhabited today.

MOSCOW, RUSSIA

One of Russia's best-known landmarks, St. Basil's Cathedral was commissioned in 1555 by Ivan the Terrible to commemorate his military victory over the Tartar Mongols. Legend has it that Ivan, even in this noble project, more than lived up to his fearsome epithet. He was so impressed with the beauty of the cathedral that he commanded its architect, Postnik Yakovlev, be blinded to prevent him from creating other buildings to rival its beauty.

Located at the edge of Red Square, the cathedral consists of eight churches capped with onion domes built around a ninth church topped by a spire that towers over them. When viewed from above, the cathedral forms an eight-pointed star, a symbol of great religious significance in the Orthodox faith. Each onion dome is unique, painted in a carnival of colors that pop out of a dreary winter landscape like so many Fabergé Easter eggs.

AEGEAN SEA, GREECE

Once a single island, Santorini's volcano erupted so violently in 1650 B.C.E. that the center of the island collapsed, creating one larger island and two smaller ones around a caldera filled with seawater. Poking up from the center of the caldera is the top of the still-active volcano. Many historians concur with Plato that this eruption was the cataclysmic event that gave rise to the myth of the lost continent of Atlantis.

At any rate, what was calamitous then is Santorini's good fortune now. Around the caldera, sheer cliffs run down to the sea. Picturesque villages of white-painted stone tumble down the sides, with the backs of many buildings reaching into the rock to form additional rooms. In some places, the roof of one building serves as the terrace of the building above or even as a narrow street. Photos of this stunning island have graced the covers of countless travel brochures, attracting visitors from all over the world.

ATHENS, GREECE

The Parthenon was built on the Acropolis, the highest hill overlooking Athens, the capital of Greece. Built to honor Athena, patron goddess of the city, it has stood since the fifth century B.C.E. despite serious damage from repeated warfare. Designed by the architects Iktinus and Callicrates, this graceful marble temple is considered to be the world's finest example of Classical Doric architecture. Knowing that straight horizontal lines tend to droop when viewed from a distance, the architects made the stepped platform bow upward, then carried the curve up through the columns, capitals, and the stonework above the columns. The combined effect produces the illusion that the temple is even larger than it is and perfectly straight. Today, the Parthenon remains the quintessential icon of the glory that was ancient Greece.

St. Mark's Basilica

The magnificence of St. Mark's Basilica cannot be exaggerated. Built in 1063, under doge Domenico Contarini, it remains the crowning jewel of St. Mark's Square. Designed in the pattern of a Greek cross laid out on a square base, the cathedral boasts five domes, the largest covering the central intersection of the arms of the cross, and a smaller dome above each of its arms. While the basic structure has remained the same, embellishments were added over the centuries. The brickwork was covered with marble and carvings, and it was rare for a Venetian ship to return from the East without bringing some extraordinary object of art to add to its opulence. One of the finest examples of Byzantine architecture, St. Mark's gilded interior is adorned with alabaster columns, ceiling mosaics, and polished marble floors with mosaic inlays of gold, bronze, and azure.

ITALY

Stretching between the towns of Positano and Vietri sul Mare, the spectacularly beautiful Amalfi coast has been prized ever since the first century B.C.E., when members of the Roman aristocracy chose to build expansive villas on the steep rocky slopes of the Lattari Mountains. For travelers, the coast was not easily accessible until 1853, when the single main road was built to connect the towns. Today, Amalfi is one of the world's most popular destinations, prized for its historical significance amid Greco-Roman ruins as well as for its rugged coastlines and sandy beaches.

PISA, ITALY

Work on the Tower of Pisa was begun in 1173 but halted only five years later when workers noticed that the free-standing bell tower had taken on a decided tilt. Work resumed in the early 1200s but stopped again in 1278. Finally, in 1360, the tower was finished and the belfry added. During and after construction, efforts were made to correct the tower's lean toward the south, which slowly increased over the years. In 1989, fearing the 197-foot-tall tower was on the verge of toppling, officials closed it to the public. By this time, experts knew the tilt was caused by unstable soil deposited by an ancient estuary. In 1999, they began gradually removing soil from beneath the tower's north side, and the tower started to straighten. By 2001, it had straightened by half a degree—enough to stabilize the structure but remain unnoticeable to viewers—and the tower was reopened.

Mont Blanc Range

The Mont Blanc massif rises up between Chamonix in France and Courmayeur, a French-speaking Italian town, which are linked by a 7.5-mile-long tunnel under the mountains. The border between France and Italy bisects the summit of Mont Blanc, which rises almost 16,000 feet above sea level and is the highest mountain in the European Alps. A glistening white dome against a fair day's azure sky makes it a particularly enticing climb for the adventurous, and about 20,000 people make the ascent each year. However, the instability of the weather can be treacherous and on peak weekends, a dozen rescue missions are mounted to rescue climbers in trouble.

Neuschwanstein Castle

FÜSSEN, GERMANY

Bavarian King Ludwig II, also known as Mad Ludwig, chose one of the world's most scenic areas to build the castle of his dreams. Begun in 1869, Neuschwanstein Castle sits high atop a hill in the Alps. The Romanesque structure, replete with medieval-looking spires and towers, was designed to look much older than it actually is. For its time, though, it was a marvel of modern conveniences, equipped with central heating, running water on all floors, and flush toilets. An opera lover and close friend of composer Richard Wagner, Ludwig had many of the rooms in the castle designed as stages for specific Wagnerian operas. One room, called the Grotto, represents a cave featured in *Tannhauser* and features artificial stalactites and even a waterfall. Of Neuschwanstein's 360 rooms, only 14 were finished at the time Ludwig mysteriously drowned in 1886. If the castle looks familiar, it may be because it was the inspiration for Sleeping Beauty's Castle at California's Disneyland.

NORWAY

Though it might seem that Thor himself had used his hammer to chisel a home of breathtaking beauty, Norway's fjords were carved not by the gods but by great grinding glaciers that covered Europe millions of years ago. Fjords can be more than a hundred miles long and thousands of feet deep. At Loenvatnet (pictured), the fjord combines gleaming masses of stone, sea, and carpets of greenery to create a landscape of unforgettable beauty.

The Alhambra

Set on a hilltop in the foothills of the Sierra Nevada mountain range, the red stone walls of the Alhambra (Arabic for "the red") hide a complex of beautiful buildings and gardens. Built in the second half of the 13th century, this brilliant example of Islamic architecture served as both a palace and a fortress during the last 250 years of Muslim rule in Spain. To cool the air, channels of water flow in and out of the palaces and courtyards with fountains. In the Court of the Lions, inside and outside are linked by intricately carved columns and arches that create a play of light and shadow that changes constantly throughout the day. It is said that while constructing the Alhambra, the craftsmen were attempting to create a physical realization of descriptions of paradise in Islamic poetry. Most visitors would agree that they had achieved their goal.

Mont St. Michel

The first monastery was built on Mont St. Michel, a rocky outcrop in a tidal bay, in the eighth century. However, the abbey perched at its peak was constructed between the 11th and 16th centuries. A masterpiece of Gothic architecture, the abbey, like the island itself, is dedicated to the Archangel Michael. Originally connected to the mainland by a thin land bridge, the abbey and the village that grew up around it were cut off twice a day by tides that raced in at over 3 feet per second. Today, a causeway provides safe passage, while parts of the bay have been reclaimed and filled in by salt marsh meadows where sheep graze. Visitors can reach the abbey by walking up a cobblestone street that winds up the hill in steep spirals.

PARIS, FRANCE

No symbol is more representative of Paris than the Eiffel Tower, named after its designer, engineer Gustave Eiffel. Constructed between 1887 and 1889, it was built to serve as the grand entrance to the Universal Exhibition, a world's fair commemorating the centennial of the French Revolution. The Eiffel Tower is 1,063 feet high, including the 78-foot antenna. Once the tallest structure in the world, the Tower was surpassed by New York's Chrysler Building in 1930. It took more than 18,000 iron pieces and 2.5 million rivets to build the Eiffel Tower, now one of the most recognized monuments in the world.

ahu   About 360 shrines on Easter Island consisting of a raised platform, a ramp, and a level court in front; some *ahu* serve as bases for moai.

bas-relief   A sculpture in which the carved figures project only slightly from their background.

Byzantine architecture   A style of architecture developed in the Byzantine Empire beginning in the fourth century and lasting until the mid-1400s; featured highly decorated churches built on the Greek cross plan, with a square central area topped by a dome and four equal-sized arms.

caldera   A large crater caused by the collapse of the central cone of a volcano, often in an explosive eruption.

chacmool   A pre-Columbian stone altar in the shape of a person lying down, head turned at a right angle, and braced on elbows with knees raised; the stomach may have been used for offerings or human sacrifices.

Dark Ages   In Europe, a period of political instability during the Early Middle Ages ranging from the fall of Rome, about C.E. 476, to 1000.

Doric architecture   The oldest style of ancient Greek architecture used from about the seventh to the second centuries B.C.E. and notable for its simplicity and beautiful proportions.

fresco   An artwork created by painting with water-based pigments on fresh plaster, which absorbs the colors so the picture becomes part of the wall.

Gothic architecture   A European architectural style, popular from the mid 1100s to the 1500s, characterized by ribbed vaulting, flying buttresses, and pointed arches that allowed for large yet open buildings; also featured large stained-glass windows.

Greco-Roman   A period of history beginning with the Roman occupation of Greece in the first century B.C.E. and ending with the fall of the Roman Empire about C.E. 476.

honeycombing   In sculpture, the process of drilling closely spaced holes in the rock so it can be easily broken apart and removed with chisels and hammers.

Inca   The largest pre-Columbian empire, centered in what is now Peru and spreading through the Andes Mountains into parts of today's Ecuador, Bolivia, Argentina, and Chile; began in the early 1200s and ended in 1533 with the execution of the ruler Atahualpa by order of the Spanish conquistador, Francisco Pizarro.

Islamic architecture   A type of architecture that includes a wide range of styles beginning with the founding of Islam in the seventh century C.E. to the present; buildings are often highly decorated with calligraphy, geometric shapes, arabesques, and mosaics.

massif   An immense, compact section of a mountain range.

Maya   A pre-Columbian civilization that stretched from today's southern Mexico south to Belize; began around 1800 B.C.E. and ended about C.E. 1541.

Romanesque architecture   A type of architecture common in Europe from the 900s to the 1100s that contained elements of both Roman and Byzantine architecture; featured massive walls with few windows and semicircular arches.

solar flare   A sudden but short-lived eruption of energy and radiation from a small part of the sun's surface.

solar wind   Charged particles, primarily protons and electrons, that stream from the sun's outer layer into space.

stratovolcano   A large cone-shaped volcano with steep sides made of alternating layers of lava, lava blocks and bombs, ash, and cinders.

stupa   A Buddhist shrine, usually with the shape of a dome.

INDEX

Acropolis, 70

Aegean Sea, 68

Agra, India, 56

Alexandria, Egypt, 3, 7
  Library of, 3
  Lighthouse of, 3, 7

Alhambra, 82

Alps, European, 78, 80

Amalfi Coast, 74

Andes Mountains, 28

Antarctica, 34

Antipator of Sidon, 3

Architecture, 3–7, 30, 44, 50, 52, 54, 58, 66, 68, 76
  Byzantine, 72
  Classical Doric, 70
  Gothic, 86
  Incan, 28
  Islamic, 56, 84
  Maya, 26
  Romanesque, 80

Arizona, 20

Artemis, 5
  Temple of, 5

Artemisia, 6

Athena, 70

Athens, Greece, 4, 70

Atlantis, 68

Aurora australis, 16

Aurora borealis, 16

Australia, 40

Ayeyarwady River, 54

Babylon, Iraq, 3, 4

Bagan, 54

Banaue Rice Terraces, 46

Bartholdi, Frédéric Auguste, 6, 10

Batok volcano, 42

Biosphere Reserve, 32

Black Hills, 14

Bodrum, Turkey, 5

Borglum, Gutzon, 14

Borobudur Temple, 44

Brazil, 30

Bridges, 18, 24, 86

Bromo volcano, 42

Buddha, 44, 52, 54

Burma, 52, 54

Cairo, Egypt, 3, 58

California, 22, 24, 80

Callicrates, 70

Callimachus, 3

Canada, 16

Canyons, 20, 28

Cappadocia, 64

Cathedrals, 66, 72

Caverns, 12

Central America, 26

Chamonix, France, 78

Chichén Itzá, 26

Chile, 32, 36

China, 50

Chrysler Building, 88

Chu State, 50

Colorado Plateau, 20

Colorado River, 20

Colossus of Rhodes, 3, 6–7

Contarini, Domenico, 72

Copacabana beach, 30

Coral reefs, 38

Corcovado, 30

Courmayeur, Italy, 78

Cuernos del Paine, 32

de Lemos, Gaspar, 30

Demetrius of Macedonia, 6

Deserts, 50, 62

Easter Island, 36

Egypt, 3, 7, 58

Eiffel Tower, 88

Eiffel, Gustave, 10, 88

Ephesus, Turkey, 5

Euphrates River, 4

European Alps, 78, 80

Fiji, 38

Fjords, 82

France, 10, 78, 86, 88

Füssen, Germany, 80

Germany, 80

Giza Plateau, 58

Glaciers, 34

Golden Gate Bridge, 24

Granada, Spain, 82

Grand Canyon National Park, 8, 20

Great Pyramid, 3, 58

Great Wall of China, 50

Greece, 4, 5, 6, 68, 70

Guanabara Bay, 30

Halicarnassus, Turkey, 5
  Mausoleum at, 3, 5

Hanging Gardens of Babylon, 3, 4

Helios, 6

Herakles, 4, 6

Herodotus, 3, 4

Herostratus, 5

Honshu Island, 48

Ibn Battuta, 7

Icebergs, 34

Iktinus, 70

Inca, 28

India, 52, 56

Indonesia, 42, 44

Ipanema beach, 30

Iraq, 4

Istanbul, 5

Italy, 72, 74, 76, 78

Ivan the Terrible, 66

Japan, 48

Java, Indonesia, 42, 44

Jefferson, Thomas, 14

Khafra, 58

Khufu, 3, 58

Koro Sea, 38

Kulkulkan, 26

Lattari Mountains, 74

Leaning Tower of Pisa, 76

Liberty Island, 10

Lincoln, Abraham, 14, 22

Loenvatnet, Norway, 82

Ludwig II (Mad Ludwig), 80

Luray Caverns, 12

Luzon Island, 46

Machu Picchu, 28

Mandraki Harbor, 6

Manitoba, Canada, 16

Marin County, 24

Marine reserve, 38

Maryland, 34

Maussollos, 5–6

Maya civilization, 26

Menkaure, 58

Mexico, 26
Moai sculptures, 36
Monasteries, 54, 86
Mont Blanc Range, 78
Mont St. Michel, 86
Moscow, Russia, 66
Mount Fuji, 48
Mount Rushmore, 14
Mount Semeru, 42
Mumtaz Mahal, 56
Myanmar, 52, 54
Namena Barrier Reef, 38
Namena Island, 38
Namib Desert, 62
Namibia, 62
National Memorial
    Mount Rushmore, 14
National Monument
    Rainbow Bridge, 18
    Statue of Liberty, 10
National Park
    Grand Canyon, 20
    Torres del Paine, 32
    Yosemite, 22
Nebuchadnezzar II, 4
Neuschwanstein Castle, 80
New York, 6, 10, 24, 88
Normandy, 86
Northern Lights, 16
Norway, 82
Olympia, Greece, 4–5
Olympic Games, 4–5
Pacific, 36
Pagodas, 52, 54
Paine Grande, 32
Paris, France, 88
Parthenon, 70
Patagonia, 32
Persian Empire, 5
Peru, 28
Pharos Island, 7
Pheidias, 4
Philippines, 46
Pisa, Italy, 76
Plato, 68
Pliny the Elder, 7

Poseidon, 7
Positano, Italy, 74
Ptolemy I, II, 7
Pyramids, 3, 26, 44, 58
Quetzalcoatl, 26
Raffles, Sir Thomas, 44
Rainbow Bridge, 18
Rano Raraku volcano, 36
Red Square, 66
Rhodes, Greece, 6–7
Rio de Janeiro, Brazil, 30
Rocky Mountains, 20
Roosevelt, Theodore, 14
Russia, 66
San Francisco, California, 24
Santiago, Chile, 32
Santorini, Greece, 68
Scotia Sea, 34
Sculptures, 4–7, 10, 14, 26,
    30, 36, 44
Seven Wonders of the World
    Ancient, 3–8
    New, 8
Shah Jahan, 56
Shwedagon Pagoda, 52
Sierra Nevada, 82
Singuttara Hill, 52
Sostrates, 7
South America, 32
South Dakota, 14
Southern lights, 16
Spain, 84
Sprinkle, Leland, 12
St. Basil's Cathedral, 66
St. John Chrysostom, 5
St. Mark's Basilica, 72
Statue of Liberty, 6, 10
Statues, 4–7, 10, 14, 30, 36,
    44
Strabo, 4, 5
Strauss, Joseph, 24
Sugar Loaf Mountain, 30
Sydney Opera House, 40
Sydney, Australia, 40
Syria, 7
Taft, William Howard, 18
Taj Mahal, 8, 56

Temples, 4–5, 26, 28, 44
Theodosius I, 5
Tokyo, Japan, 48
Tombs, 3, 6, 56, 58
Torres del Paine National
    Park, 32
Towers, 76, 80, 88
Turkey, 5, 64
Underground structures, 64
Universal Exhibition, 88
Urubamba River, 28
Utah, 18
Utzon, Jorn, 40
Venice, Italy, 72
Verrazano-Narrows Bridge,
    24
Victoria Falls, 60
Vietri sul Mare, Italy, 74
Volcanoes, 36, 42, 48, 64, 68
Wagner, Richard, 80
Washington, George, 14
Waterfalls, 22, 60, 80
World's largest
    Buddhist temple, 44
    curtain of falling water, 60
    manmade structure, 50
    musical instrument, 12
    natural bridge, 18
    sculpture, 14
Yakovlev, Postnik, 66
Yamuna River, 56
Yangon, Myanmar, 52
Yosemite National Park, 22
Yosemite Valley, 22
Yucatán Peninsula, 26
Zambabwe, 60
Zambia, 60
Zeus, 4
    Statue of, 3, 4–5
    Temple of, 4–5

IMAGE CREDITS

WONDERS
OF THE WORLD

A Virtual Tour in 3-D

Text by Mary Packard

Image Selection by Linda Falken

BARNES & NOBLE

NEW YORK

Front cover images clockwise from top right: Golden Gate Bridge, Moai Sculptures, Great Wall of

China, Sydney Opera House, Grand Canyon, Santorini, Machu Picchu, St. Basil's Cathedral

Back cover image: Sydney Opera House

Image credits on page 94

Designed by Alisa Komsky

Images converted to stereo by Tim McCulloch and Ryan Paola at MAGroup, Bethel, CT

ISBN-13: 978-0-7607-9180-6

ISBN-10: 0-7607-9180-5

Printed and bound in China

1   3   5   7   9   10   8   6   4   2